BY THE FYRE

Collected Poems from the Heart of the WYLD

By Amethyst Wyldfyre

~W~

Wyldfyre Communications Press

Copyright @2016 by Amethyst Wyldfyre

Published and distributed in the United States by:

Wyldfyre Communications Press

122 Hills Ferry Road, Nashua, NH 03064

www.wyldfyrecommunications.com

Cover Design by Amethyst Wyldfyre via Create Space Template

Printed by Create Space

All Rights Reserved. No part of this book may be reproduced by any mechanical, photographic, or electronic process or in the form of a phonographic recording, nor may it be stored in a retrieval system, transmitted or otherwise copied for public or private use – other than for "Fair use" as brief quotations embodied in articles and reviews without prior written permission of the publisher.

The author of this book does not dispense medical advice or prescribe the use of any technique as a form of treatment for physical or medical problems without the advice of a physician either directly or indirectly. The intent of the author is only to offer information of a general nature to assist in the quest for spiritual well being. In the event that you choose to use any of the information in this book for yourself, which is your constitutional right, the author and the publisher assumes no responsibility for your actions.

By The Fyre - Collected Poems from the Heart of the Wyld / Amethyst Wyldfyre

February 2016

ISBN 13:978-0-9821189-6-2

ISBN 10:0-9821189-6-1

Printed in the United States of America

DEDICATION

To James – Child of my Heart – Thank you for coming to teach me how to feel and how to grow.   Nothing is stronger than the love that we share. Nothing.

And for Amanda – Sister Friend – Soul Family – Thank you for reminding me that writing – the real kind – is essential to the wellbeing of my soul. You my dear are a very Good Win!

FOREWORD

I'm a messenger. Let me just be clear with that both for you and for myself. As a messenger I feel it's my sacred calling to transmit the message. Regardless of the packaging, the message - the energetic transmission - the vibration of my intent is incorporated and infused for the purpose of activating and awakening something within the receiver.

I speak, I write and I make art. Sometimes I package my art in a wrapping paper that is meant to get it in under the door. Sometimes I let my art be revealed in all it's naked glory. Either way the only act I am here to perform is to be the channel.

Today I want to write - about writing. I want to honor the muse within. The messenger angel that whispers into my ears with all kinds of whispy inspiration - the turn of a phrase, the cadence of a poetic paragraph, a catchy title, perhaps even a tune. I want to write about this angel - and my role in our relationship. You see the message.....it comes from that greater field of energy that is the bigger part of me (and you too). The celestial and the terrestrial co-conspiring to bring forth INSPIRATION. I am a channel. It's my job to be clear. Unobstructed. Roto-rootered so that nothing but the purest essence of the message is brought through. My only job - other than to be clear is to say YES PLEASE I will transmit thank you. It's not my job to make sure you read. Or listen. Or become activated. Because the truth is - some will, some won't.

I write because I must. (I must I must I must increase my bust....... I remember that little poem from when I was an adolescent - as a side note - there wasn't anything that I did - even repeating this poem multiple times that actually increased my bust - but here it is still with me! - Thanks to the writer/channel/poet who brought it through and delivered it into this realm - the words were engrained in my psyche.)

Words are magical, mystical, magnetic and mesmerizing when well-crafted and truly great art is really crafted in the beyond and then delivered - through a channel - to the world. I cannot take credit for anything other than being open, willing, able and committed to channeling the messages through. I can enjoy however the satisfaction that comes with bringing it up, and out. With the completion of the thought - the riding of the flow - the sparkle of making words come to life on a page. I can revel in the delight that I feel when another person reads my words - and better yet "Gets" the message.

Truth is there is only one single message I am here to deliver. Replace Fear with Love.   That's it. That's all she wrote.   And yet How do I Love Thee? Let me Count the Ways......

I love thee - and me - enough to challenge myself to return to my Source - the infinite well of wisdom and write. As much as I can, every day - no buts about it. Starting today. I write. Because I'm a messenger. That's why.

Amethyst Wyldfyre
in a gift of love to myself
Valentine's Day 2016

We Begin……

The Flow…..

Writing - For Your Life

Sometimes the flow just has to go.....
Regardless of what "those people" might think.

The writing is urgent
Like a bum needs a drink.

I have to indulge it and see where it lands
even if sometimes it's written in sands.

When I write I am able to be with the Source
the words from the heavens and my heart of course.

I must let it flow or I surely will die
the pressure inside of living the lie.....

Will blow up my heart and make it stop beating
If shut down the writing it's like I stopped eating.

Sometimes I hear the angels my friend
they tell me the message and ask me to end

The suffering inside and all around me
by letting the words out so others can see.

I write for MY LIFE because it's so clear
that writing is what brings my angels quite near.

They whisper and moan when I turn them away
If I shut down the writing they no longer play

So write for your life because that's where it starts
when you translate to words the vibes in your hearts.

The words are like magic as they dip and they soar
Bringing joy into sorrow and ceiling to floor.

Remember the beauty and let it come out.
Write on my soul siStars it's your turn to shout.

Love note…..

Words....... Matter.........

They do - it's true.

Words....... Matter........

To me and to you.

When I speak the words that hurt your heart.
They slice right through like a poison dart.

When I speak the words that are my sacred truth I revel in joy at the incredible proof......that

Words...... Matter.......

When the flow is strong and my head is hot
the words that land can create a knot

Between us both that is hard to untie
Especially when....... my words are a lie.

This happens sometimes when I am in pain
I seek for the other on whom I lay blame.

And then I discover the damage of course
I have to make my way back to the Source.

Because Words........ Matter.........

When the flow is strong and my heart is aflame
I create a connection that's more like a game.

We can play with each other and laugh with delight and maybe face off in Scrabble all night!

Where my words and yours overlap and we score with words that are golden and some that are poor.

But every one counts in the end don't you see.
Because these words are connecting the you with the me.

I love you my dear the meaning's quite clear. I am grateful to know that your heart also hears, and remembers.......... Words....... Matter.

Empty Staircase…..

White Noise

White Noise fills the space between my ears drowning out the sounds of the crying baby

and the creaking of the bed in the next room.

The staircase outside my bedroom is quiet now & solitude my only companion

as I sink into the bedding and make a feeble attempt to fall asleep.

The sounds of no thing not even my own heartbeat seems able to penetrate the static

of white noise thought forms about what could have been if only.....

I had been somehow better.

Magnetic poetry….

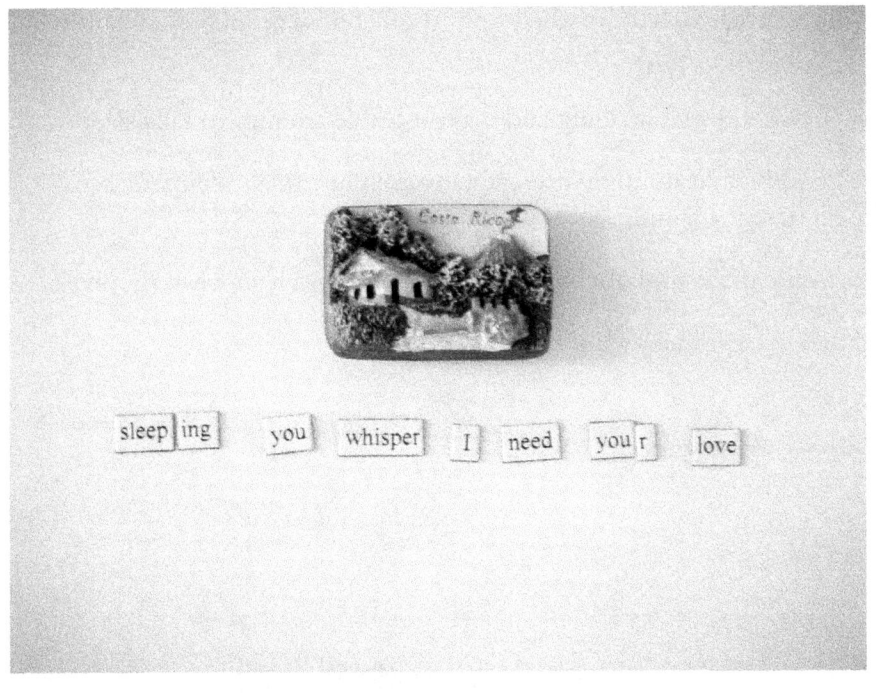

Poetry

Poetry is soothing to the core of my being

For it is only with this language are we able

to remotely touch the vastness of Spirit

& the Great Mystery of the Inner Worlds.

Come with me as I journey to faraway lands, ancient times

to the center of a flower or the warm steady breathing of a newborn

sleeping at his mother's breast.

Painting with words I quest

To be able to more fully express

the depth of emotion I feel

without spilling too many tears on the page

and smudging the sacred stanzas that hold......

......if you pause and allow them to touch you.......

a magic that can not be found

in the whizbang technology that is here today & gone tomorrow

and a very poor substitute for the depth of connection

that your heart longs to make with the heartbeat of the world.

Let these words awaken your desire to live and love again
in all the messy, tasty, delicious and perhaps even dangerous ways

you were born to explore.

Walk away from the multi-colored GodGrid of computing functions

and DANCE with my words playing beautiful music on the heartstrings of your soul.

Divine Nature......

Outside the Lines

I Like to Color Outside the Lines

Of the empty boxes we put around ourselves

Decorated with mascara & lipstick and layers of fancy clothing and high heeled shoes......

Packaged to disguise the truth of who we are to appease

The Gods of manufactured housing who like us to eat cardboard replicas

of what once may have resembled food.

The mind overflowing with images chosen, songs sung, and words spoken

to keep the fear alive and separate our souls from our natural state of aliveness.

And when my coloring is done I shall go outside and scream in ecstasy at the radiant rays

of sun setting over clear waters in the far away hidden places where Nature is still divine.

Tree Being....

I Breathe

In through the nose, out through the mouth

I breathe.

Taking in life force,

ancient air once breathed by dinosaurs

and recycled a trillion billion times or more

through every imaginable creature to ever walk

the face of this Earth.

In a moment of insight

my breathing stops short

and I gasp

at the vastness and elegance

of the Divine Plan

As I take a deep inhale

at the base of a majestic tree being

and wonder......

am I breathing you?

or are you breathing me?

Flowers Blooming…..

Awakening

Light dawns in the dim recesses of a mind in turmoil.
A faint glimpse of another way.   Distant yet clear.

Guides arrive to support the journey, like flowers blooming
on a garden path.

Are you my teacher? My student? Ah yes!!! The Divine Paradox!
We are for each other.... Both, And.

Thank you for showing me all the forgotten hidden aspects
of your Divinity.   Create yourself anew.

The Awakening

Is NOW.

Kitty Love…..

The Cat in the Window

You watch with those sharp azure eyes
the swirling leaves scattering down the sidewalk
pushed by the winds of change.

Your ears alert to the sounds of passing cars
and the rusty chain on the neighbor boy's bike
as you seek to hear again the footsteps of the one
you love the most, bounding up the stairs and
slamming the door behind him.

To swoop you in his arms, bury his face in the
softness of your neck and sigh with pleasure
at the pure unconditional love that emanates from you
as you purr with delight at the smell and the sight.

Kitty Love it may be a while before you see that smile
but don't you worry because I will tend to you
as you sit and patiently stand guard on the windowsill
observing the Earth turning slowly
and the days passing by.

The Door…..

Open

the door and let in the light.
The letter on my table waits.
Words fail to express
the depth of my sorrow.

Moments shared pass through my mind
as I sit and stare with blank eyes
and a heavy heart.

Wondering.......
Could I have done more, been better,
spoke truer, loved harder?

Oh I know this is a fruitless set of questions
only designed by a mixed up mind
to torture me into believing
that it's all my fault.

I must not allow them to take hold.
For if they do the open space will close
and there will be room left for no one to enter
and nothing left to lose or choose.

One breath at a time and with the remembrance
that thoughts create I erase this poison
from my thinking.   And pray.
For my faith to be strengthened
and my heart to stay

No Matter What..........

Ever Open.

Birds Take Flight…

When I Write

Birds take flight
In patterns of black
On a sky blue day
Filled with radiant light
When I write.

Beauty emerges as the words unfold
Of times and spaces that I have yet to behold
The poetry that lives in me comes out
For all the world to see
When I write.

I paint with words a vision clear
Of all the things that I hold dear
Like harmony & peace & joy
And spending time with my little boy
When I write.

If I hold back when the verses come
I lose the connection to the Source they are from
And my heart starts to hurt and my head starts to ache
Truly there is so much at stake that must come through
Into written form for that's the way a Vision is born
When I write.

Word Painting....

I Am A Poet

I Am a poet.
Sharp with the pen.
A master of painting with the written word.

I feel the flow of Universal Wisdom
pouring down my arm as the purple ink flows
making marks between the lines.

Between the lines of words on the page
is the essence of Love and Beauty
Harmony and Peace
that emanates through my being as
the phrases pour forth.

Sometimes rhyming
and at others a flow
of unrelated words that somehow merge together
to create an impression meant to touch, open,
activate and delight.

The Source of all is on this page
and as you read my poetry
the lines enter into your beingness
and stir an ancient future memory
of the timespace when you too would say

I Am a Poet

and the people would bow in gratitude
for the wealth of wisdom that you poured forth
from your lips
and your fingertips.

Moonlit Night....

Breathing Light

A Magical night where the stars were shining
and the truth was dining on the false promises made
by those in the shade
who know not the glory of the unfolding story
of Earth and the Sun and the stars dance of delight....

Are you Breathing???
Breathing Light?

When I sing and open my heart
to the magic of music and rhyme
that bubbles through my being
desperate to find

it's way out of me and into the world
to be heard and received
I have to remind myself
with the question....

Are you Breathing???
Breathing Light?

All about me dancing under the stars
the faerie beings and elven ones
the unicorns and magical mavens
who cast the spells to enchant and delight

the human kind who know not the powers
they hold themselves to create and play
in the Divine Matrix of delight.

Are you Breathing???
Breathing Light?

Poetry and Art and Song and Dance!
Remember NOW is our only chance
to laugh and play and enjoy the sight
of the shimmering stars on this Moonlit night

Are you Breathing???
Breathing Light?

About the Author

Amethyst Wyldfyre is a multidimensional visionary. Her work spans the globe as she serves women of wisdom everywhere to channel their wisdom, welcome wealth and change worlds.

She speaks, writes, performs miracles and makes magic wherever she goes and loves to dance with faeries and snuggle with Jack the Corporate Cat as often as possible!

She's the creatrix of the Crystallize Your Message Laboratory Intensive™ an 8 week virtual experience that serves messengers who want to become clear and empowered to bring their blessing to the world.

She also leads visionary Return to the Source™ Retreats for Women of Wisdom in fun and fabulous sacred locations around the world (and sometimes in her backyard!)

Find out more and apply for enrollment for either of these offerings here:
http://www.theempoweredmessenger.com/map

Her signature homestudy Money, Magic & Miracles Clarity Course for Empowered Messengers™ has helped hundreds (on the way to thousands!) of people to create a more meaningful, magical, and miraculous relationship with money so that they are able to enjoy feeling like they have more than enough every day all the time and are able to finally leave their money worries behind for good.
Find Money, Magic & Miracles here:
http://www.moneymagicmiracles.com

You can book her to speak either live or virtually by visiting her speaker site here: http://www.amethystwyldfyre.com

For direct inquiries by phone dial 603-594-2744 or write directly to the author & publisher at amethyst@amethystwyldfyre.com or by post to
Amethyst Wyldfyre Enterprises, LLC
122 Hills Ferry Road
Nashua, NH 03064

www.ingramcontent.com/pod-product-compliance
Lightning Source LLC
Chambersburg PA
CBHW070952180426
43194CB00042B/2476